JUST
COINCIDENCES?

A village Pastor's amazing stories

John Richards

Just Coincidences? A village Pastor's amazing stories.

British Library Cataloguing-in-Publication Data
A catalogue record for this book is available from the British Library.

ISBN: 978-1-915283-00-9 (Paperback)
ISBN: 978-1-915283-01-6 (Epub)
ISBN: 978-1-915283-16-0 (Mobi/Kindle)

PERMISSIONS

All persons named in this book have given the author permission to do so.

NOTE ABOUT SPELLING

British spelling (e.g. centre, cheque, and 'for ever' as in the RSV translation of the Bible) has been used throughout.

Print information is available on the last page.

BOOKS FOR LIFE TODAY
86a Totteridge Lane, High Wycombe, HP13 7PN, England
Email: sales@booksforlife.today
Website: www.booksforlife.today

Foreword

Pastor John Richards and I began our ministries in Buckinghamshire at the same time.

John, in his ministry, had three outstanding qualities which shine through the pages of this book. He had a total belief in the truth of God's Word, and in particular the teaching of Jesus himself; he was open and willing to be led by the Holy Spirit, even when he didn't understand why; and he had a love for people, such that he rarely failed to share with them the truth of the gospel whenever he had the opportunity.

Each of the 29 stories John has recorded suggests on its own that God was supernaturally at work, but when they are all put together it is hard to come to any other rational conclusion.

John has since retired, but my prayer is that through this book his evangelistic ministry will continue to bear fruit until Jesus returns.

Rev Arnold V Page. BSc, BD, MIWSc

Just Coincidences?

Preface

I had been a member of the Elim Pentecostal Church in the Buckinghamshire village of Lane End since my conversion in 1972. I studied theology at the Elim Bible College in Capel, Surrey, from 1976 to 1978, and became the pastor of the Lane End Church in 1981.

I want to thank my wife, Marion, for her loyal support, encouragement and faithful commitment to me over the years.

In this book I share some of the events that I have experienced during my pastoral ministry, the purpose being to glorify God, as well as to bless and encourage you, the reader. There are those who will always deny the supernatural, but I ask you this question: "Could all the events in this book be just coincidences, or could they be due to the involvement of One who said, 'I am the Resurrection and the Life', of whom it was written, 'There are also many other things which Jesus did; were every one of them to be written, I suppose that the world itself could not contain the books that would be written.'? (John 21:25)

Just Coincidences?

Contents

Preface vii

Introduction 1

Divine healing 5

The Kingdom of God is righteousness and peace and joy in the
    Holy Spirit 7

Take delight in the Lord, and he will give you the desires of your
    heart 9

Jesus said, "Give, and it will be given to you." 11

The gospel is the power of God for salvation 13

Sons of the King 15

Jesus said, "I will build my Church." 17

"In my name they will cast out demons." 19

My God will supply every need of yours according to his riches in
    glory in Christ Jesus. 21

An inner prompting of the Holy Spirit 23

Where is the God of Elijah? 24

A Japanese wedding in Lane End 25

I commend to you our sister Phoebe 27

There is power in the Name of Jesus 29

Bind the Strong Man 33

Call to me and I will answer you 35

Chrissie the Christian 37

In everything God works for good with those who love him 39

Love thy neighbour 41

Don't let the devil in 43

"Therefore I tell you, whatever you ask in prayer, believe that you
    have received it, and it will be yours." 47

"You shall have no other gods before me." 49

He cares 51

Chosen people 52
I am the Lord your healer 53
Off to the Philippines 54
He got rid of the Buddha! 55
The blind blind man 57
Conclusion 59
Further reading 61

Introduction

'Whoever calls on the name of the Lord shall be saved.' (Acts 2:21)

I was born and spent my childhood in the Cornish village of Par, where my family regularly attended the local Primitive Methodist Church. As a child I found church very boring, but I now know that the faithfully committed Sunday School teachers sowed precious seed, God's word, into my life. I must have assisted in their own spiritual progress, for 'suffering produces endurance '(Romans 5:3), and as a boy I certainly was a cause of considerable suffering to them!

My wife, Marion, was an Anglican, who had been confirmed at the age of sixteen. Twelve years later when she was on her way home from a church service, she met her friend Margaret. On hearing that Marion had just been to church, Marion asked her if she was a Christian. "Of course I am", she replied, "I've just been to a church service." She was surprised to hear Margaret reply, "That doesn't mean you're a Christian. We have a young minister lodging with us, perhaps you would like to meet him?" The minister, Len Magee, was the pastor of the Elim Pentecostal Church in Lane End, near High Wycombe. On meeting him, Marion said, "Well, as you're a preacher, I suppose you should preach to me!"

Pastor Magee was quite taken aback by this, and arranged an appointment to see Marion the following day, when they duly met. The pastor read a passage from Isaiah chapter 53, and then shared the gospel with her. Marion, in tears, knelt and received Jesus Christ as her Lord and Saviour.

On returning home, she was full of joy and talked to me about being saved and becoming a Christian. I said that I thought she already was a Christian, but she insisted that she had just received Christ and had been born again. In the days that followed, Marion tried hard to share the gospel with me, but I was having none of it! As far as I was

1

concerned, I didn't mind her attending church meetings, as long as she didn't expect me to go.

Unbeknown to me, my wife had approached the prayer group at the church, saying that as wild horses wouldn't drag me into church, would they please pray for my salvation. Their prayers proved to be effective!

A little later, Marion asked me if some friends could come around one evening. I had a high-powered job, which I really enjoyed, but which left me very little time for friends. When I found out that my wife had invited the pastor, I objected to the point of threatening to throw him out, but after being assured that he wouldn't preach to me, I reluctantly agreed that he could come.

I was very surprised when I met him because he was completely different to what I had expected. I later discovered that everyone who was there that night, with the exception of three of us, was a Christian. Little did we know that within a few days the three of us would also be born again!

During the evening, I virtually chain-smoked, and I must have bored everyone stiff showing our holiday movies and talking about myself. The pastor kept his word and didn't preach, but I told him that I couldn't believe the Bible, as it was full of contradictions. To my surprise, I was even able to point a few out to him. He very graciously explained that the seeming contradictions arose because I had taken the verses out of context.

I then suggested to him that if he were honest, he would admit to being afraid of death. This was a problem that had plagued me personally throughout my life. The Christians laughed and assured me that they did not fear death, as they had received eternal life.

The evening ended and I could neither understand nor believe, but I was very much aware that they had something that I did not have. Later I was to learn that the something they had was actually someone, the Lord Jesus Christ, who came 'to deliver those who through fear of death were subject to lifelong bondage.' (Hebrews 2:15)

A few days later, whilst driving to work, I was caught in a traffic jam. Some very impatient people were sounding their car horns and shouting abuse. I remember asking myself, "What is life really all about?" It seemed just then to be something of a pointless rat race, and I felt in despair. I had lovely wife, two beautiful daughters, a new detached house, a new car and a good career, but... There was definitely something missing in my life.

As I eventually drove on, I decided to talk to God. I said, "I cannot believe what those Christians told me about you, that you even know the number of hairs on my head. If you know that much about me, then you must know me better than I know myself. Therefore, you must know that I cannot believe, so if you are real, please help me to believe."

It was a cry from deep within, and as it left my lips, I stared in amazement. I had regularly driven along that road, but never before had I noticed a large stone cross, which I was now driving directly towards. I was oblivious to everything else around me. I cried out, "Jesus, forgive my sins and come into my life." Immediately, I could see! It was an instant conversion and from that moment my life changed forever.

I was instantly aware that everything was different. I later discovered these words in a hymn: 'Something lives n every hue Christless eyes have never seen.' I knew what the hymn writer meant. Jesus said "Behold, I make all things new."(Revelation 21:5) New desires, new friends, new principles to live by. Was it just a coincidence that I happened to be in that particular place at that time? I think not.

Thank you Jesus for saving me. Thank you, Marion and the Church, for praying for my salvation. Little did they realise that not only would God save me, but would give me to the Church as their pastor to serve Him and them.[1]

---

[1] The stone cross is at a road junction in the village of Bisham, Buckinghamshire. Engraved on it are the words 'Jesus my Redeemer'.

Divine healing

'Is any among you sick? Let him call for the elders of the church, and let them pray over him, anointing him with oil in the name of the Lord; and the prayer of faith will save the sick man, and the Lord will raise him up...' (James 5:14-15)

Fifty years ago I had a small growth under my left eye. It was about the size of a pea. It wasn't a serious condition, but it did require an operation to remove it. Being squeamish I absolutely dreaded the thought of an operation around my eye. We were singing a hymn towards the close of a church service, and my mind was on the annoying growth, when suddenly the word of God came to me: "Call the elders of the church to pray for you."

The congregation were still singing when I walked to the front of the church, fully resolved to call upon the elders. But before I could do so, the Pastor and a visiting Baptist Minister walked up to me with a container of oil. I protested that I had intended calling them to anoint me and pray for me, in obedience to God's Word, but they had not given me the opportunity. The Pastor assured me that God knew my intentions. They proceeded to anoint me and pray for me.

I returned to my seat, complaining to God that I had not been given the opportunity to actually 'call' for them exactly as the Word said. The congregation again sang the last verse of the hymn they had been singing when I had walked to the front, and then the meeting was closed in prayer.

I felt for the lump under my eye... it was gone! As far as I am concerned, God had fulfilled his Word and performed a miracle.

The immediate disappearance of a growth that had required an operation to remove it. Was this just a coincidence? Or was it God's power at work?

Just Coincidences?

The Kingdom of God is righteousness and peace and joy in the Holy Spirit (Romans 14:17)

While attending a week's Elim Church Conference with my friend, Dennis Court, we saw God answer many prayers. One in particular concerned the conversion of Elaine. We arrived at the camp and were carrying our luggage from the car park, when we passed some chalets for the residential staff. A poster in one of the chalet windows caught our eyes, and out of interest we paused to read it. It referred to seeking 'peace and joy'.

Each morning we had spoken to a young assistant at a confectionary kiosk. Her name was Elaine, and she came from Newcastle. Each day we had invited her along to the evening service. All our invitations were politely declined, and there seemed to be no likelihood of a positive response. However, near the end of the week and to our surprise, Elaine said she would like to attend a Christian coffee bar meeting, and we agreed to take her.

Dennis and I sought the Lord together and asked that in some special way he would speak to Elaine. There was some time to spare before the coffee bar meeting so we took her to look around a missionary exhibition. The last display stand had photos of a city, with a caption that read, 'This could be your city'. Elaine stood there for some time saying nothing. We asked her if something was wrong, to which she replied, "This *is* my city, Newcastle."

In the coffee bar, Elaine received Jesus as her Saviour. Afterwards, the three of us walked around the camp. Without understanding very much of what had just happened, Elaine was baptized in the Holy Spirit and started speaking in tongues!

We accompanied her back to her chalet, and on arriving discovered that hers was the chalet with the poster we had seen in the window on our arrival at the camp. It was her poster! She had found in Jesus Christ the peace and joy she had been seeking.

Was seeing the poster, meeting Elaine, and all that ensued just a series of coincidences? Or was it the work of the Holy Spirit?

Take delight in the Lord, and he will give you the desires of your heart
(Psalm 37:4)

We had a wonderful time at the Elim Bible College Open Day at Capel in Surrey, but as I observed all that took place I felt rather sad. My pastor, Len Magee, noticed this and asked me what was wrong. I told him how disappointed I was that I had not been saved at an earlier age, as I would love to have studied at the College. I had become a Christian at the age of 32 and now had the responsibility of taking care of my wife Marion and our two small daughters, Catherine and Alison.

My pastor said that nothing was impossible with God, and that if I delighted myself in the Lord, he would grant me the desires of my heart! I took this scripture to heart and communicated my desires to the Lord.

This was all very much in my thoughts when, just two years later, I walked up the driveway of the Elim Bible College with my wife, our very dear friends Keith and Marian Ingram, and my suitcases. God had fulfilled his promise to give me the desires of my heart, and I was about to attend the College for the next two years. Was this God fulfilling his word... or just a coincidence?

Perhaps you too have a long held desire. If so, may I suggest that you also 'delight yourself in the Lord', so that he may grant you the desires of your heart as well.

Jesus said, "Give, and it will be given to you." (Luke 6:38)

While attending the Elim Bible College in Capel, Surrey, I was given special permission to return home to my family every weekend. I was glad that another student was able to give me a lift, as I had not been able to obtain a grant and therefore didn't have much money.

On one occasion, the student giving me a lift told me that he had no money, and his car needed urgent repairs over the weekend in order so that he could return to the College from his home in Wales. He had obtained a quote for the repairs and I winced when he told me the cost.

We drove to a garage for some petrol, and while he attended to this, the Holy Spirit clearly prompted me to give him the money he needed. My thoughts flew to my wife, Marion, who was working part time in a glue factory. She would have to work for ten weeks to earn the amount my friend needed. Then I realised that I didn't have my chequebook with me and I felt a sense of relief! Yet I still sensed the Holy Spirit prompting me to pay the man. I then remembered that in the side pocket of my holdall was a cheque that I kept for emergencies. I wrote out the cheque and gave it to my friend. It was a joy to hear him praise God.

When I returned home and told Marion what I had done, she also praised the Lord without hesitation!

Marion and I told no one about this, but during the course of the weekend someone anonymously posted an envelope through our letterbox. There was no letter in the envelope, just money. When we counted it out it was exactly double the amount I had given to my friend!

Receiving money through our letterbox never happened at any other time during my two years at Bible College, and we never had the slightest idea who was responsible for this gift.

Was this just a coincidence? What do you think?

The gospel is the power of God for salvation (Romans 1:16)

Towards the end of my two years at the Elim Bible College I sensed the Holy Spirit prompting me to go and preach the Gospel from John O'Groats to Land's End. As I shared this with my wife, Marion, it all seemed a bit silly. I remember telling her that I didn't even know the distance, and I decided to dismiss the whole thing.

I sat back in the chair and switched on the television. To my absolute astonishment I found myself watching a programme about a man on crutches who was doing a sponsored walk from John O'Groats to Land's End! The commentator even gave the distance of the walk! Just a coincidence?

On leaving College I set off for John O'Groats with a fellow student, Wally Waldeck from South Africa. We decided we would get there first, and then commence preaching. However, just before we left home, we were asked by a Christian lady to stop at Princes Risborough in Buckinghamshire and visit her friend who was very ill, in order to share the gospel with her. This we did, but sadly the gospel seemed to fall on deaf ears.

On returning we did have some wonderful testimonies to share, but when someone asked me how many people had been saved I had to say I had no idea. I had simply preached the gospel and moved on. Later, I reflected on this and prayed, "Father, I would love to have seen some of the fruit from our labours." Within minutes I received a phone call from the Christian who had asked us to share the gospel with her friend in Princes Risborough. She asked me if I would visit her friend again as she had become gravely ill and was now in hospital.

I went there that evening and found the poor lady to be so ill that I wondered if she would even be aware of my presence. A nurse informed me that she would probably live no more than a few weeks.

I was uncertain whether or not she would hear me, but I decided to share the gospel with her again. She was evidently in agony, but all of a sudden she became very still. Then she sat up in the bed and simply said, "Jesus", with a look of wonder on her face. No longer in pain, she lay back again with a radiant look.

Until then she had been unable to sleep well, but this time she closed her eyes and fell asleep. Her friend wept softly, and we both believed we had witnessed a miracle of salvation. I prayed for the lady and asked the Lord to take her to be with himself. Then we left. We later learned that she had never opened her eyes again.

Later, I reflected on what I had said to the Lord about desiring to have seen some fruit from the labour. This dear lady, now in the Lord's presence, had been the very first person we had shared the gospel with on our preaching tour!

Sons of the King

My friend Wally and I were driving through the Scottish Highlands heading for John O'Groats. The weather was atrocious - dark with heavy rain. Our camper van roof leaked, and as a result our bedding was drenched. To make matters worse a red warning light was flashing on the dashboard indicating a problem with the engine. It was all very depressing, and I found myself asking, "Did God really call me to do this?" I could have been warm, dry and comfortable at home with my family.

As I pondered all this, I remembered that I had been informed of a Christian retreat centre where we might find some hospitality. I reached for the map and searched to see where it was in relation to our current location. Thankfully, it was nearby.

The Kilravock Castle was owned by the Rose Clan and was situated in a valley near the River Nairn. On our arrival we were met at the door by a butler. We briefly explained who we were, and that our intention was to preach the gospel from John O'Groats to Land's End. The butler asked us to wait, and went off into the castle. He soon returned with a lady who informed us that she was the Chief of the Rose Clan. On learning about our mission, she welcomed us in and invited us to stay. We were shown to a delightful room at the top of the castle, a welcome contrast to spending a night in the back of a leaking camper van!

There were a number of other Christians staying at the castle, and we enjoyed an evening of fellowship with them. Later on, as I relaxed in a steaming hot bath, I was warmed more by the thought of how gracious the Lord was to lead us to such a place as this. We were very blessed, and had truly been treated as Sons of the King!

The Rose Clan's enthusiasm for the gospel is reflected in a stone plaque on the outside of the wall of the west courtyard. It bears the following inscriptions: 'Non est salus nisi in Christo' - 'There is no salvation except in Christ'; and 'SOLI DEO GLORIA', - 'TO GOD ALONE BE THE GLORY'.[2]

---

[2] Here is some of the history of Kilravock. William Kilravock II was knighted by King Robert the Bruce and fought in the great victory over the English at Bannockburn in 1314. Mary Queen of Scots stayed there in 1562. Bonnie Prince Charlie stayed there just prior to the nearby Battle of Culloden. Queen Mary visited Kilravock in 1922.

Jesus said, "I will build my Church."
(Matthew 16:18)

When we arrived in the small Scottish town of Fort William, my friend and fellow evangelist Wally and I were told that a Mrs Sarah Macbeth would accommodate us. When we arrived at her house she welcomed us and said, "This must be of God." She attended a small United Free Church of Scotland, and the minister was away for that weekend. The Church had prayed that the Lord would send someone to preach in his absence, and now two preachers had arrived on her doorstep!

She told us that local churches were banning Pentecostals from the pulpit. People were being told to have nothing to do with them and to burn their books. There were, however, a number of people in different churches in Fort William who had been baptized in the Holy Spirit.

On the Sunday, Mrs Macbeth told the congregation that God had answered their prayers and provided two people who would minister - one in the morning and the other in the evening. She introduced us, and explained that we were from a Pentecostal Bible College! During the evening service, a man began to shout praises to God, an unprecedented act in that United Free Church of Scotland!

We later talked with Mrs Macbeth, who agreed to contact all the people who had been baptized in the Holy Spirit, inviting them to a meeting that we had arranged to hold in the Caol Community Centre. About twenty people came: the praise and worship was beautiful, and the gifts of the Spirit were exercised.

It was a lovely occasion. There was immediate unity among the people, even though they came from very different church backgrounds. One old gentleman informed us that he had been a deacon in the Church of Scotland for many years, but when his minister denounced the baptism in the Holy Spirit, he felt he could no

17

longer continue to worship there, having already been baptized in the Holy Spirit for quite some time. Another couple had moved to Fort William from Cheddar in Somerset, believing that God had led them there to join a new work. God's timing is perfect, and it is no coincidence that we arrived in Fort William on that particular weekend. God cannot be restricted or overruled!

We left Fort William with its own brand new Pentecostal Church.

"In my name they will cast out demons."
(Mark 16:17)

While attending the Elim Bible College I was asked to preach on Sunday evenings at a hired hall in Maidenhead. Very few people attended the service, but each week a young man named Norman came, always smelling of drink. Usually my wife and our friends Margaret and Dennis would take the young man for a coffee after the service.

One evening when I was at home, Dennis rang to tell me that Norman had turned up at his home. He was returning to Glasgow, his home town, and was the worse for drink. Dennis asked me to go round to his house. We sat with Norman, who had a large bottle of whiskey with him. We talked to him, and suddenly he began to say some very dreadful things about Jesus on the cross. I had never heard anything so evil. He was so abusive it was obvious there was a demonic problem.

Margaret left the house in a hurry and went to join my wife at our home. Norman began to abuse us verbally and vile language poured out of his mouth. He wanted to beat me over the head with a poker! Normally I would have fled, but surprisingly I felt no fear whatsoever. As he came towards me like a fiend I pointed a finger at him and commanded the demon in the Name of Jesus to leave him. At the very mention of the name Jesus, Norman fell to the floor as if someone had hit him over the head with a baseball bat.

I told him to repent and receive Jesus, and he began to weep and pray for salvation. The next moment he was weeping for joy, and he poured his whiskey down the sink! I felt exhausted and asked Dennis to read from the Word of God. He just opened the Bible and read these words: 'The man from whom the demons had gone begged that

19

he might be with (Jesus); but he sent him away, saying, "Return to your home, and declare how much God has done for you!'"

Norman had come to tell us that he was returning home to Glasgow the following day. Dennis and I took him back to Maidenhead, gave him a Bible and took our leave of him, never expecting to hear from him again.

Two years later on our preaching tour from John O'Groats to Land's End we reached Glasgow. I told Wally about Norman and we prayed for him. Glasgow is one of the largest cities in the UK and I had absolutely no idea of Norman's whereabouts. We parked our van and walked to a shopping centre.

I knew that in Maidenhead Norman had worked for an electric company, so seeing an electric shop I thought I would go in and see if they had heard of him. I hesitated, thinking it would be a waste of time, but then decided I might as well go in and ask. I spoke to an assistant explaining that I wanted to contact a man named Norman Walker. She replied, "Oh, Norman. He's over there." I turned around and Norman and I were facing each other! He was now a manager, with a wife and child, and no longer had problems with alcohol. We enjoyed lunch together, and although I have never seen or heard from him again, I know he is in God's safe keeping.

I was absolutely astonished at what had happened. I believe this was more than just a coincidence. What do you think?

My God will supply every need of yours according to his riches in glory in Christ Jesus. (Philippians 4:19)

After I graduated from Bible College I returned to regular work with my old company. Three years later, I resigned in order to commence serving the Lord as the full-time Pastor of the church in Lane End, Buckinghamshire.

While I was working my notice some of my colleagues asked what I was going to do regarding transport, since I had had the use of a company car for the previous three years. I decided to ask the Lord about it. While praying about it, I had a clear vision of a particular car - a red Cortina. I believed it was mine, so I excitedly ran downstairs to tell my wife that we had no need to be concerned about transport, as God was giving us a red Cortina.

As my leaving date approached, I was asked by the company to hand over my vehicle to another company on the last day of my employment. I asked what would happen to the car which my current car was going to replace, and I was told that it was to be sold. I immediately asked the make of the car, and was told it was a Cortina, a red Cortina! So I asked if they would be kind enough to provisionally put my name against it, as I was interested in buying it. The car had just been completely overhauled and it had brand new tyres. The company who owned it had spent £500 on it before deciding to sell it for £500! Christian friends had already contacted me to say that they were prepared to spend a total of £1500 on a car for me, so my buying it was no problem.

On the afternoon of my departure from the company, I stood in the office with some of my colleagues and I reminded them of what I had told them – that my new employer, God, was going to supply me with a red Cortina. I asked them to look down into the car park, where I pointed out to them my red Cortina, the keys to which I had just received. God's timing is perfect!!!

I said my farewells and drove off, not in a green Rolls Royce or a yellow Mini, but in a red Cortina. I gave thanks all the way home: the vehicle had cost me personally nothing at all.

Was the provision of my new car and the timing of my ownership of it just a coincidence, or was it the supernatural result of answered prayer?

An inner prompting of the Holy Spirit

One morning while sitting in my office at the church in Lane End, I sensed an inner prompting of the Holy Spirit directing me to go to the nearby town of High Wycombe. On the way there I said to the Lord, "I have no idea what you want me to do. I'll park my car and walk around the town, and if you haven't told me what to do, I'll head back to my car and drive back to the church." But I truly believed that God had a purpose in sending me there.

I parked my car and walked around the town centre. Standing near the Guild Hall, I looked across at the Parish Church and the Holy Spirit prompted me to go inside. It is quite a large church; I sat by an aisle and looked around.

At first I thought the building was empty, but then I noticed a man sitting at the front. The Holy Spirit instructed me to tell him that Jesus wanted him to preach the gospel. I walked up to him. He looked at me and I duly delivered the message: "Jesus wants you to preach the gospel." The man began to shout praises to God! He told me that he had a desire to serve the Lord in evangelism, and had sat there praying for God to send a man to confirm that this was God's will for him.

Anyone would be hard pushed to believe that this was just a coincidence. What do you say? Just an amazing coincidence? Or God truly at work?

Where is the God of Elijah?

I was experiencing some difficulties in my pastorate, and I began to wonder if I was serving God in the right place. We had hit a particularly barren time spiritually in the church; we had not had any new converts for a very long time, and I was cast down in my spirit.

I walked up to Wheeler End Common on an extremely wet and stormy day. In a howling gale, I began to call upon the Lord. "Lord, it's been such a long time since we've seen anyone saved. Will you confirm that I am in your will, serving you where you would have me to be at this time?"

I was pouring out my spirit to the Lord, when I decided to 'lay a fleece'. I asked the Lord for three converts from the village in the next week. I had an assurance in my spirit that this would happen, and I went home with a spring in my step, wet and dishevelled but praising Almighty God.

The following day I was in my office at the church when there was a knock at the door. A young lady came in and said that she wanted to become a Christian. I led her to the Lord and praised God, thinking that this was the first of the three converts. Later that same day I had the joy of leading a couple to Christ. I was later to marry the couple and baptize them in the River Jordan in Israel.

I thanked the Lord that after having seen no converts for such a very long time, I had the joy of seeing three, and the very next day!

A Japanese wedding in Lane End

I received a telephone call from a Mrs Iwanaga, a director of the Euro-Japanese Exchange Foundation in the village. She rang to ask if I would be willing to officiate at the wedding of a young Japanese couple. The wife-to-be was still in Japan, but she and a number of guests who had practically no knowledge of the English language would shortly be flying into the UK.

According to Mrs Iwanaga, the couple were of a Buddhist background but the young lady's parents had been converted to Christianity, and she specifically desired to be married in a Christian church.

Arrangements were made concerning the date and time, etc. The wedding was to be on a Saturday afternoon.

In church on the preceding Sunday morning, I noticed a young oriental lady in the congregation. I thought she might be someone from the Euro-Japanese centre who had come to talk to me about the wedding. After the service she told me that she was indeed Japanese, but knew nothing whatsoever about the wedding and was just visiting. I explained about the wedding due to take place the following Saturday, and I asked her if she might be able to assist me. She willingly agreed to do so.

I wrote out everything that was to be said, and the Japanese lady summarised it, placing little marks where I should pause so that she could interpret it effectively. During the week we decided to obtain Bibles in Japanese for the couple and the best man. We managed to obtain two Bibles by the Friday of that week, and although they were from two different sources they were identical.

The lady also taught me how to welcome the bride, groom and guests in Japanese. Unfortunately, despite my best efforts on the day, everyone just stared at me with puzzled expressions. However, it was a beautiful wedding, and the bride and groom, Mr and Mrs Miyamoto, have since sent me a photograph of Baby Miyamoto.

What amazed me was that, apart from the wedding, this was the only time to my knowledge that a Japanese person had attended a Sunday service at the church. It wasn't three months before the wedding, or six weeks after, but the very week that we needed a Japanese interpreter. What is also remarkable is that the young lady, who so readily and graciously assisted me, disappeared after the wedding. We never did know where she had come from and we never saw her again.

Hmm! Was this just another coincidence? Or did God send special help for the wedding arrangements?

Letter of thanks received from Teniko Iwonaga

Thank you very much for arranging a very good wedding ceremony for Mr and Mrs Miyamoto. I would be most grateful if you could convey our sincere thanks also to the Japanese lady who interpreted your address beautifully.

I commend to you our sister Phoebe (Romans 16:1)

I received a telephone call asking me to visit a young Nigerian lady who had lost the will to live. She had broken her neck in a traffic accident in Nigeria and was quadriplegic. She was being cared for at The Paddocks Hospital in Princes Risborough.

I sat at her bedside and tried to have a conversation with her, but she was totally unresponsive. I decided to read her Psalm 23, and as I was reading I heard her say, "Hallelujah!", after which she began to converse with me.

About six months before, her husband had been killed. His neck had been broken in a traffic accident, and she was left a widow with two small daughters. She became a Christian, and then she had the accident. Her neck was also broken, and although she had survived, she had been left paralysed. She told me of the longing of her heart to return to Nigeria to be with her daughters, who were then in the care of her parents. She also said that she would love to meet someone who could speak the Hausa language and communicate with her parents.

I said to her, "If, instead of giving up, you delight yourself in the Lord, He will grant you the desires of your heart." (Psalm 37:4)

"I will," she replied.

On returning home, I related what had happened to my wife, Marion. She suggested that I call the Wycliffe Translation Centre at nearby Horsleys Green. A lady answered the phone. I told her of my meeting with Phoebe, and how we were trying to find someone who spoke the Hausa language. The lady got very excited and shouted down the phone, "This is of God!" She had a young Nigerian staying with her by the name of Joshua. He too had broken his neck in a car accident in Nigeria, and he too was quadriplegic. He had received treatment and was returning to Nigeria in a few days' time. And yes, he spoke the Hausa language!

I made arrangements to collect Joshua and take him to see Phoebe. As I collected him from the Wycliffe Centre and was putting his wheelchair into the boot of my car, a young man came running up to us, shouting to Joshua. He had only just arrived from Nigeria but he readily agreed to come with us, so I headed to the hospital with not one, but two Hausa-speaking Nigerians!

When we arrived, I went to see Phoebe, leaving the others to arrange for Joshua and his wheelchair to be taken upstairs. I asked Phoebe if she had been 'delighting herself in the Lord', and she replied that she had been. So I said to her that God had already started to respond, as not one but two Hausa-speaking Nigerian Christians had come to see her!

The young Nigerian pushed Joshua in his wheelchair to Phoebe's bedside and then... pandemonium broke out! I could understand some show of emotion, but this seemed to be way over the top. They all seemed to be shouting at once. The reason was that the two young men both KNEW PHOEBE! They had come from the same village, and the sister of the young man who had joined us was Phoebe's close friend!

After this meeting there was a great change in Phoebe. She started attending our church and began writing letters by holding the pen between her teeth. One day, some weeks later, Marion and I took Phoebe, two wheelchairs, and heaps of medical supplies to Heathrow Airport, from where she flew back to Nigeria to be re-united with her daughters. The Lord had granted her the desires of her heart.

There are over 150 languages in Nigeria and over 500 million people. Which do you really think is more likely? A set of astonishing coincidences, or God-answered prayer?

There is power in the Name of Jesus

Our church building was situated about half a mile outside the village of Lane End, a village which has a population of about 3,700 people. The building lay in beautiful surroundings, but was isolated from the life of the village and its housing estates.

Through the commencement of a children's work in the village, we saw that there were great needs, which gave us the vision to build a new church in the heart of the community. We prayed much for a particular plot of land that was on the very edge of the housing estates. It was a quarter of an acre in size and it belonged to the County Council.

We wrote to the Council a number of times, but were told that the plot was reserved for the building of a library. Nevertheless, we continued to pray for it.

One day, I was walking on the piece of land, asking the Lord to allow us to have it to build a new church there, when someone called out to me. It was a lady whose three children attended our children's club. She asked me if we had obtained the plot yet, as she had heard of our intention to build a new church there. I explained to her that we did not, as yet, own the land, but that I had just been praying for it.

I went on to explain to her that the building would be used by 'the Church', and that 'the Church' consisted of Christians, described by God as 'living stones'. I began to share the gospel with the lady, and informed her of her need to receive Christ. Her response was that she could not do this. I was reminded of what Jesus said, that if you would plunder a strong man's house, you must first bind the strong man. So I did it. I bound the devil in the Name of Jesus Christ and loosed the woman. She immediately responded to the gospel and received the Lord Jesus Christ as her Saviour! We were both filled with joy. Jesus was already answering our prayers to build his church there. This newly saved lady had become a 'living stone', having received Christ on that very piece of ground.

It was then that I knew without a doubt that the land was ours. Regardless of what anyone said, a church was destined to be built there. On the Sunday, I announced to the church that the land was ours. Shortly after this my daughter, Alison, had the joy of leading a young man to Christ on that same plot of land.

After I had made the statement concerning the land we still got no further with the council. Some time later, in a meeting I attended with my son-in-law, a Nigerian preacher named Benson Idahosa shared how he had sought God for a quarter acre of land on which to build a church. He went on to tell us that people said he was wasting his time, but he believed there was power in the Name of Jesus. Benson prayed and trusted in God, and he got the land by approaching the authorities in the Name of Jesus. We were amazed and excited, as what he had related to us was just what we wanted to do.

We decided to write again to the County Council, and this time we wrote at the foot of the letter, 'in the Name of the Lord Jesus Christ of Nazareth.'

We received an immediate reply from the Chairman of the Council. He said there was a possibility of selling the land to us, and he arranged for the church treasurer, Roy Pitcher, and me to meet the Land Evaluation Department. We were told that the value of the land was £100,000. Our immediate response was that we couldn't afford such a sum, but would consult with the Church and get back to them. After prayer, we made an offer of £25,000... and it was accepted!

The District Council then informed us that to grant permanent right of access to the land across the existing car park they would require £12,000. Again, we prayed about it and our offer of just £1,000 was also accepted! The land was ours, the church was built and before long it was fully paid for.

We give all praise and glory to our Heavenly Father for our beautiful church building. There is power in the Name of Jesus!

Were the unexpected salvation of two people on the prayed-for plot of land, the testimony of Benson Idahosa, the change of heart by the Council, and the acquisition of the land and the access to it at such greatly reduced prices, all just coincidences? I think not!

Just Coincidences?

Bind the Strong Man
(Matthew 12:29)

I was preaching the gospel and handing out tracts in the city of Plymouth. I noticed a young woman sitting nearby: she had been sitting there for some time. I felt I should talk to her, so I asked her if she was enjoying the sunshine or listening to the gospel. She replied that she was in fact doing both.

Although she was wearing sunglasses I could see that she was crying, as tears were flowing down her face. I asked her if she would like to talk to me. Nodding, she proceeded to tell me that she was married with two small daughters, and her husband had been a high-flying city businessman. However, he had decided to give up the city career and purchase a retail business in Basingstoke. All the changes had affected her husband and had put him under so much pressure that he had become impossible to live with.

The young woman continued to cry. She told me that as a result of these events she had left him, moved to Plymouth with her daughters, and had opened a ballet shop. It transpired that she was a Christian, and although her husband wasn't he had always attended church services with her.

I gave it some thought and offered to visit her husband in Basingstoke once I returned home. I kept my promise and made an arrangement to visit him after his business closed for the day. Despite being very polite, he explained that he felt there was no point in talking to me. However, I was not going to give up. I explained that I also had two small daughters and, like him, I had been in business and understood the pressure he was under. I also told him that his wife had said both she and their children loved and missed him very much. After this I shared the gospel with him.

Once again he said that I was wasting my time. He said 'it had never happened for him'. When I asked what he meant, he said that he had never fallen to the floor when people had prayed for him! At this point I prayed a silent prayer, for I knew the Lord had led me into this situation and I needed his guidance. I recalled again Jesus's instructions to bind the strong man, and I knew then what to do. I bound the devil and loosed the man in the Name of Jesus. At once he started to sob and he received the Lord Jesus Christ as his Saviour.

A week or so later I called the young woman. I was delighted to hear that she and her husband had been reunited, they were living in Plymouth, and all was well.

What a wonderful Saviour is Jesus my Lord!

Call to me and I will answer you

I was sitting at home with my wife, watching a television programme, when the words, "Go and see David McClenaghan" seemed to flash through my mind. I dismissed the thought but it came back again, and again and I dismissed it. The thought came yet again, and this time and I took it to be the prompting of the Holy Spirit. I shared it with my wife, who said, "You will have to go, but be careful."

We didn't know David, but had heard that he could be violent. David answered the door. He invited me in and I began to share the gospel with him. He said that he had noticed men from the church and that he would like to be like them, but could never see this happening to himself. I shared with him that God was able to do this for him and that he needed to receive the Lord Jesus Christ. David said that he could see what I was saying but he just felt unable to repent and turn to God.

I told him to sit there and ignore what I was about to do. I was led by the Holy Spirit to bind the devil and free David from his control. (See Matthew 12:29) I bound the devil in the name of the Lord Jesus Christ and loosed David. He immediately received Jesus as his Saviour.

The next morning, David went to see his mother, a member of our fellowship, to tell her that he had been saved. At first she thought he was messing about, but he assured her that it was true. Beryl was amazed, because the previous evening she was on her knees before God concerning her son. The problems with him had been so great that she felt she couldn't take any more. Weeping before God, she had handed him over to the Lord.

Could the timing of this have been just a coincidence? That a wayward son was saved by the grace of God on the very same evening that Beryl had handed him over to the Lord? Great is our God, and greatly to be praised!

Chrissie the Christian

A member of one of our midweek evening house groups had invited two Filipino sisters, Chrissie and Maria, to join us. Both ladies seemed very low, and they explained to me that Chrissie had recently been diagnosed with terminal cancer. Chrissie went on to explain that she was a Roman Catholic, and her husband, Ron, was a Welsh Presbyterian. Apparently, she and Ron argued incessantly about religion.

Chrissie and Maria told me that they had a niece in the Philippines who was 'one of the born again', and they were unsure what this meant. I gave them a brief overview of the meaning of salvation, that Jesus Christ, the Son of God, had died and risen again and by doing so had paid the penalty for the sins of mankind. I explained that anyone who calls on him for forgiveness and acknowledges Jesus as Saviour is 'born again' into the spiritual realm and receives a new life.

They were both overjoyed, for it transpired that they believed and had prayed this prayer with their mother some time before. The penny dropped and the term 'born again' was understood. As this realisation dawned on them their previous mourning turned into great joy. (Jeremiah 31:13)

After this, both sisters attended our church regularly. Chrissie was baptized in the Holy Spirit and received the gift of speaking in tongues. Chrissie's husband Ron came to see me, eager to have what his wife and sister-in-law had received, and he too was born again. Now there was no more arguing over religion, but total unity in their family instead. Chrissie had been a born-again Roman Catholic and had not realised it. Ron was a Welsh Presbyterian who had thought he was 'alright', but he actually needed to be saved. Now the dividing walls were down and they were truly one. What joy there now was in that home, despite how serious Chrissie's cancer had become!

Some months later Chrissie was taken very ill and I received a call from Ron asking me to go to their home. When I arrived Chrissie had just passed away. Maria told me that Chrissie had held out her hands to Ron and herself, and whispered "Jesus." Then she had died.

One morning soon afterwards Ron came to see me, expressing a desire to learn more about the Lord. He wanted to have some 'one to one' Bible teaching, which we agreed to start on later in the week. Then he left, as he had some business to attend to in the town.

That afternoon I received a call from Maria. Ron had collapsed and was in hospital. Both Maria and I sat with him, but he never regained consciousness. Ron died on the day that he had expressed a desire to know God more. That very day his journey was over, and his desire was made complete.

In everything God works for good with those who love him

(Romans 8:28)

I was approaching a junction with a main road. Seeking a break in the traffic to my right I made the mistake of assuming that the car in front of mine had already moved onto the main road. I moved forward and crashed into it.

The driver of the other car was a young woman who was in a hurry for an appointment, so she asked me to write my name and other details on a piece of paper. I wrote down my initial and surname and she said, "I didn't ask you to write *my* name. Anyhow, how did you know my name?" I assured her that I had written my own name. It turned out that we had the same initial and surname!

Then she said, "Don't I know you from somewhere?" I looked at her and realised that I too recognised her from somewhere. We then remembered that many years beforehand we had lived across the road from each other and our families had been very friendly. I had even led her parents to the Lord. We examined the damage to our cars and went our separate ways. Her name was Julia, and she was later to relate to her family our very odd way of meeting up!

At that time, Julia's brother Jonathan had a young Christian friend named Maria. She had only recently become a Christian and had not yet joined a church fellowship. When Julia told Jonathan about the accident, he remembered me too, and recalled that I was a pastor and had built a church in Lane End, which was only about three miles from where Maria lived. He decided to take Maria to a Sunday afternoon service.

He later admitted that when the service commenced with praise and worship he hated it and wanted to leave. However, he stayed, heard the gospel and was converted. By the end of the service, he was joining in the praise himself!

Jonathan and his parents became members of the church, as did Maria, her husband and her mother. Jonathan's father became an elder in the church. His sister Nikki and her husband Steve were also saved and they too joined the fellowship. Steve became a deacon and their two daughters, Charlotte and Lizzie, are now also both saved.

At the time of the accident, who could have foreseen the many events that were to follow? But then, 'In everything God works for good with those who love him, who are called according to his purpose.' (Romans 8:28)

Love thy neighbour

Our near neighbours, Geoff and Jean, had four children, three daughters and a sixteen-year-old son, Geoffrey.

One day, a few years ago now, we were told that Geoffrey had been rushed to hospital in London, as he had been taken seriously ill. The details were a little sketchy, but later that day I was informed that the doctors had said there was nothing that could be done, and it was likely that Geoffrey was going to die. On hearing this, I called the church to a special prayer meeting, and at this meeting we called on the Lord for a miracle of divine healing.

A few days later, while on my way to church, Geoff approached me. He was very excited and told me that there had been a 'miracle': his son was going to live after all. I explained to him that the church had gathered together to pray for Geoffrey's miraculous healing, and Geoff was flabbergasted. It transpired that the doctors had had to remove a quarter of Geoffrey's skull in order to relieve pressure on his brain. After this major operation Geoffrey had returned home. Some months later he returned to the hospital to have his skull reconstructed. The medical staff were still concerned that he might not live a normal life, due to the fact that the treatment had all been so close to his brain. In fact Geoffrey was fine, and to this day he has led a normal and fulfilling life.

Some years later, Geoff came to see me at the church. He had become very ill himself, and had decided that it was time for him to sort his life out and get right with God. I was delighted to share the gospel with him, and as a result he received the Lord Jesus Christ as his Saviour. The miracle of healing that Geoffrey received was awesome, but the miracle of salvation that his father received was even greater. Geoff's sins had been forgiven; he had been reconciled to God, and had received eternal life. With God ALL things are possible.

Just Coincidences?

Don't let the devil in

Shortly before I became a full time minister, I had an experience that taught me much about the wisdom of God. I had been at work all day, and on arriving home Marion told me she had received a phone call from a woman who was threatening to take her own life. I called the woman, and she reiterated that unless I met her immediately she would commit suicide!

I arranged a place to meet her, but feeling rather unsure about the situation, I asked a neighbour, Derek, who was a new convert to Christianity, if he would come along with me. When we arrived at the meeting place I asked Derek to wait in the car while I got out and waited in the place where we had arranged to meet. A short woman with a whippet dog approached me. I immediately felt terribly uncomfortable, and more so as the woman related her life story to me.

She was the child of Satanist parents who had offered her to Satan as a sacrifice. A self-confessed drug addict and lesbian, she was in need of accommodation and she insisted that she should come and stay in my home. She added that if I refused I would be like the priest in the parable of the Good Samaritan, who had crossed over to the other side of the road to avoid helping the injured man. Again she threatened to commit suicide.

At this point it began to rain, so I suggested that we went to the car to take cover. When the woman saw my friend Derek in the car, a torrent of curses spilled out of her mouth, and she demanded to know what he was doing there. Then she said she would call me the following day, when she would expect the accommodation in my home to have been sorted out for her.

Derek, our wives and I prayed about the situation. Afterwards I knew what I had to do. When the woman called next day, I made it clear that she would not be staying at my house, and furthermore I wanted nothing to do with her. Despite her threat to commit suicide and what seemed like a very un-Christian thing to do, I felt great peace and knew that I had made the right decision.

The woman had mentioned that she had previously stayed with a vicar and his wife in Oxford. I decided to investigate further and called a vicar I knew of in Oxford. This man had written books on demonic deliverance and I felt he might know of the woman. The vicar's wife answered my telephone call and I gave a brief overview of what had happened. After a pause she told me I had done exactly the right thing.

It transpired that it had been this particular vicar and his wife that the woman had stayed with. She had wrecked their home, been violent, and had attacked a doctor. It had taken six men to get her out of the vicar's home. Their belief was that the woman was a possessed servant of Satan, whose ministry was to wreck the lives of ministers and their ministries. It had taken this experienced vicar many weeks to get his ministry back on track after the woman had finally left.

I was so relieved and thankful to God. Here was I, about to start out as a new minister in a full-time role, and the devil had attempted to ruin God's plans.

That evening, I was sitting at home feeling relieved and at peace, when I had an inner prompting of the Holy Spirit to immediately visit the vicar of my sister-in-law's church on the other side of town. When I arrived, the vicar, Dennis, had friends visiting, and though he welcomed me into his home I could sense that he was wondering why I was there. I felt awkward and told the Lord as much as I sat and smiled, sipping my tea. A little later, when I felt sure I had more than outstayed my welcome, the doorbell rang.

It was about 11 p.m. One of the group of friends answered the door and came back saying that there was a woman at the door to see Dennis. Immediately, I knew why I was sitting there. "Does she have a whippet dog with her?" I asked. The friend confirmed that this was the case. I told Dennis to have nothing to do with her and to send her away.

Once she had gone, I related what had happened to us earlier. Dennis was aghast. He told me that he was about to embark on a ministry of evangelism! The plans of the devil had been thwarted, and we all praised the living God together.

Just Coincidences?

"Therefore I tell you, whatever you ask in prayer, believe that you have received it, and it will be yours."

(Mark 11:24)

The wedding that Saturday was a lovely occasion. I noticed that Julie, a single mum, was there with her little son John, who was happily playing with the other children. So I was shocked on the following Monday to receive a phone call from her to say that John had been rushed to Great Ormond Street Hospital in London, because he had been diagnosed with cancer in a kidney.

John underwent an operation, and one of his kidneys was removed. Shortly after this he had a second operation, when it was discovered that he also had cancer in his remaining kidney. The situation seemed hopeless. John was transferred to a hospital in Amersham, and when I visited him there the little boy was just skin and bones, with tubes and wires protruding from all over his body. There was nothing anyone could do.

I returned home with a sense of righteous anger, coupled with compassion for Julie and little John. I called a special prayer meeting at the church, and it was well attended. We met for the sole purpose of praying for John's healing. I asked everyone to get fully involved and to call on God, reminding them of the scripture, "Call on me and I will answer you and show you great and mighty things which you have never seen." (Jeremiah 33:3) The church responded, and I believe it was the noisiest prayer meeting I have ever attended. We all called on the Lord.

After a while, the meeting suddenly became silent, and during the silence, we made a statement of faith. We truly believed that it would be well with that little boy, despite the fact that his condition looked so hopeless. We then stood and thanked and praised the Lord, again a very noisy time.

John made a complete recovery, and his healing has withstood the test of time. He is now a father of two sons and he lives a completely normal life.

Coincidence... or miracle?

"You shall have no other gods before me."
(Exodus 20:3)

Blanche was one of our more elderly church members. Rhoda was her dear friend of a similar age, who had recently become a Christian through Blanche's witness. Blanche had taught Rhoda thoroughly, reminding me of a mother hen nurturing her chick.

It was during one of my visits to Rhoda that she expressed a concern that she had not yet been baptized in the Holy Spirit. She was puzzled about this, as she had become very close to the Lord and was earnestly praying for this enrichment of her Christian life. I pondered what she had told me while Rhoda went into the kitchen to make some tea. When she had gone, I glanced around the room, and there in her fireplace, smiling up at me (or so it seemed) was a small statuette of a Buddha! All at once, things became clear to me.

When Rhoda returned with the tea tray, I explained that this effigy had no place in the home of a born again believer. She was aghast and asked me to get rid of it. I took it away, and when I returned to my home I chopped it in half and threw it in my dustbin with a shout of "Hallelujah!"

On Sunday, Rhoda excitedly told me that she had been baptized in the Holy Spirit and was now able to speak in tongues. I asked her when this had happened, and she replied that it had been about half an hour after I had left her house. It was the same time that I had destroyed the graven image!

He cares

As I sat in my car waiting for the traffic lights to change, I saw a woman waiting at a bus stop. I sensed the Holy Spirit prompting me to tell her that Jesus loved her. Thoughts rushed into my mind, "I can't do it. She's a complete stranger!" It was a very busy road and it was difficult to pull in opposite the bus stop, but I stopped the car, wound down the window, and called to her, "Jesus wants you to know that he loves you."

She called back, "Thank you very much."

About two years later, I was invited to speak one evening at an Anglican house group. I knew one or two of the people, and I thought I recognised a lady, but I couldn't remember where we had met. She felt the same and a little later said to me, "You're the man who called out to me that Jesus loved me, while I was waiting at a bus stop." I told her that I had felt a bit stupid at the time, yet I believed that the Holy Spirit had prompted me to do it.

She related to me that at that time in her life she was a believer going through a severe trial, and her faith was at a very low ebb. She said that my calling out to her was a turning point, and that it was precisely what she needed to hear at the time. We praised and thanked the Lord together.

Chosen people

While officiating at a funeral service, I noticed a couple in the congregation who were clearly distressed. Les and Linda were a well-known couple in the community. I didn't know them well, but I knew of them. Les had spent time in prison throughout his life for various offences. As I looked at them in their distressed state, I was moved with compassion. The following day at the church prayer meeting I asked the group to pray for Les's and Linda's salvation.

The day after the prayer meeting, I was working in my office when there was a knock at the door. I was astonished to see Les standing there. Church was the last place Les would normally be seen. He grabbed my arm and said that he didn't know why he had come, but felt he had to. No sooner had I asked him to take a seat than there was another knock at the door. This time, it was Linda. As she entered the office, both Les and Linda looked at each other and enquired in unison, "What are you doing here?"

Once the shock of each other's presence in my office had worn off (both their shock and mine), I began to talk to them about the Lord and his love for them. I prayed for them both, bound the devil and loosed them in the Name of Jesus. At once, they both received the Lord as their Saviour.

I am the Lord your healer
(Exodus 15:26)

Julie had led a tempestuous lifestyle. In her mid-twenties she was wonderfully saved, and, as in everything she does, she was fervent in all her ways. Sadly, after three years of following the Lord, Julie slipped back into the ways of the world. Her enthusiasm for the things of the world was unfortunately just as fervent. After this, we rarely saw her at church.

One afternoon many years later, we received a telephone call from the General Hospital in High Wycombe. Julie had been taken ill while on holiday abroad, and because of the seriousness of her illness she had been flown back to the UK by air ambulance. She was unable to retain any fluids, and when we arrived at the hospital she was in the cardiac ward. We were shocked to see her so poorly, but as we had been called to visit her we decided to anoint her with oil and pray for her healing. After praying for her we left, feeling very concerned.

The following day was a Sunday, and as usual Marion and I were up early, getting ready for the day ahead. At 8.00 a.m. the phone rang. To our amazement it was Julie! She was excited and shouting down the phone that she had been healed, discharged from hospital, and would be at church later that morning. So much for my faith! You could have knocked me down with a feather!

True to her word, Julie arrived at the 10.30 am service. As soon as she stepped into the building she broke down sobbing and vowed never to backslide again. She went on to worship with her husband, Owen, in our church along with her daughter Teri, her son-in-law Keith (Teri met Keith at the church), and her little granddaughters, Grace and Beth, who were both dedicated to the Lord.

What a mighty God we serve!

Off to the Philippines

A large group of churches in the Philippines had linked up with the Elim denomination in Britain. Some of the Elim ministers, including myself, were asked to visit the Philippines to hold teaching seminars for the church leaders there.

One of our church members, Maria, came from the Philippines, so I rang to ask for any helpful advice that she could offer me. Maria's husband, Alan, answered the telephone. I explained to him the reason for my call. Alan was amazed at this because he had been praying concerning his own future. He was a qualified engineer, but the desire of his heart was to serve God in the Philippines! Alan's wife, Maria, had been saved since leaving her native Philippines, but since then she had had no contact with any evangelistic churches there.

I needed to know if the Lord wanted me to travel to the Philippines, so I 'laid a fleece'. I said, "Lord, if you want me to go please supply the means for me to travel there." About an hour later, before I had left my desk, a lady came to see me. She had heard that I'd been asked to go to the Philippines and had spoken about it to her husband. As a result, they had decided to pay for all eight of my flights, insisting that I travelled with Singapore Airlines, which they considered to be the best.

I was still sitting at my desk in shock when another lady came to the office. She handed me a small packet that she had been asked to deliver to me. It contained £500 in new £5 notes! There was a note enclosed that just said, 'to help towards your expenses in the Philippines'. The Lord indeed wanted me to go!

During my visit to the country I was able to talk to the church leaders there about Alan and Maria, and the leaders were able to help them get established when the couple eventually arrived in the country.

He got rid of the Buddha!
Exodus 20:3

A young couple had recently joined our church, and I visited their home. As I waited for them to answer the door I noticed a statue of a Buddha in the garden. When I mentioned to the young woman my concern about their having a Buddha, she explained that it belonged to her brother, so she couldn't get rid of it but she had refused to have it in her home.

On the following Sunday the couple came to church. They brought with them the woman's brother Joe (who owned the Buddha statue), and another brother, Frederick. On talking to Frederick after the meeting, he told me that he was involved in evangelism in London. He also said that he had visited our church once before, and he remembered that I had preached on 'binding the strong man'. I had referred to the scripture where Jesus said, "If you will plunder the strong man's house, you must first bind the strong man."

(I've mentioned in earlier chapters how, when sharing the gospel, some people seem unable to respond to God's command to repent until one has bound the devil and loosed them from his control, when they are immediately able to receive the Jesus Christ as Lord.)

As we were talking, Joe came and asked if he could sit with us, and we invited him to do so. He said, "My sister told me what you said to her about my Buddha. I want you to have it and do what you want with it."

I said to Joe, "You have heard the gospel and have been unable to respond," and he agreed.

Turning to Frederick, I said, "You can now see what I have been telling you about."

I bound the strong man in the name of the Lord Jesus Christ and I loosed Joe. Immediately, he wanted to pray and to receive Jesus Christ as his Saviour. God had demonstrated to Frederick the power of his Word.

Could it have just been a coincidence that when I bound the devil and loosed Joe he was able to do what he had not been able to do before, or was this indeed the outworking of the power of Almighty God as he promised in his Word?

The blind blind man

Every morning I would take my laptop and briefcase to my car and drive to the church. One morning, however, I decided not to take them, or the car. Instead I started to walk around the village.

On reaching the village centre, I wondered why I was doing this. I stopped and asked God if he wanted me to do something in particular. I had an immediate response - I call it an inner prompting of the Holy Spirit. "Go and see the blind man."

I knew that the blind man lived in a cottage in the direction I was heading for, but I didn't know his actual address. I found a house called 'The Cottage' and tried knocked on the door. It was opened by the blind man. I told him who I was and he invited me in.

We proceeded to talk, and he told me about his life in the village and how he had lost his sight some years before. I asked him if he would agree to go through a survey of four questions with me, and he readily agreed.

The first question I asked him was whether he attended a place of worship, and he replied that he had always attended church until a few years ago.

I asked him if he believed in an afterlife. "Definitely," he replied.

I then asked him if he understood how the cross of Jesus Christ related to him personally. I thought he would have understood, but to my astonishment he said, "I have no idea at all."

My final question was, "If you died today, and God asked you why He should let you into heaven, what would you say?" His response was, "I have always tried to live a good life and I have always helped anyone in need."

I told him that I knew what he was saying was true, because I had heard it said in the village what a kind and generous man he was.

"Now, while this is commendable", I told him, "the good life you have led can never get you into heaven, for we cannot be saved by our good works."

I then explained to him the relevance of the cross: that we can never be good enough, and that is why Jesus died on the cross for us. He paid the penalty of our sin, which is death, and by receiving him as our Lord and Saviour we become born again and receive eternal life.

Suddenly, the blind man leaped from his chair with his arms outstretched and cried out, "I can see for the first time in my life!"

He now understood how the cross related to him. I prayed with him. He acknowledged that he was a sinner, and that Jesus had died on the cross for him, and he received Jesus as his Saviour.

As I walked home, I realised I never did get to the church! I'd had no need of my laptop or my briefcase. Instead, I had had an unforgettable morning. Was it just a coincidence that I decided to walk to church that day? I think not! The blind gentleman was 98 years old; he had attended church throughout his life, yet had never understood the gospel until that morning!

Conclusion

What are we to conclude about 'Just Coincidences'? Either these experiences of the pastor of a small village church are simply remarkable coincidences, or else Jesus Christ is real and is very much alive! Christians all over the world can testify of similar remarkable incidents, probably running into tens of millions. The truth is that Jesus Christ has indeed risen from the dead. He is the Resurrection and the risen Saviour of the world; he is alive now and will be for evermore.

I find it astonishing that whilst we still claim to be a Christian country there is such a widespread lack of understanding of how the cross of Jesus Christ relates to us personally. So for those who still do not know, I will endeavour to explain...

Sin is the great problem of the whole human race. Everyone has sinned, and sin separates us from God, from Heaven and from each other. We are born with a body, soul and spirit, but the spirit is dead because of our sinful nature. This is why Jesus says, "You must be born again or you will never see or enter the Kingdom of God." (See John 3:3)

Many people believe that they will go to Heaven because of the good things they have done. Good deeds are of course commendable, but they will never get anyone into Heaven.[3] You must be 'born again'!

How is man's problem of sin resolved? Only through faith in Jesus Christ. Jesus said, "My blood is shed for the forgiveness of your sins." Jesus, by dying on the cross, paid the penalty of sin for all who believe in him. We have to come to Jesus, acknowledging that he died on the cross for us. We receive him by faith as our Saviour and the new Lord

---

[3] Editor's note: Whilst most people think of Heaven as somewhere above the clouds, the Bible makes it clear that everyone saved by faith in Jesus will eventually live for ever in a newly created <u>earth</u>. See Matthew 5:5; 1 Peter 3:13; Revelation 21:1-4.

of our life, and in so doing we receive forgiveness of sins, new birth, and the precious gift of eternal life. There is no other way. This is the gospel (good news) of the Lord Jesus Christ. Jesus said, "I am the way, and the truth and the life; no one comes to the Father, but by me." (John 14:6)

John Richards has since retired from active ministry. He worships at the New Life Christian Fellowship, which meets at Studley Green Community Centre near Stokenchurch on Sundays at 10:30 am.

Elim Hope Church in Lane End is now led by Pastor Scott Pash. We meet for worship every Sunday morning at 10:30 am, and you are welcome to join us in person or via Zoom. A link is on the website.

The street address is Elim Hope Church, Edmonds Road, Lane End, High Wycombe, HP14 3EJ, United Kingdom.

Telephone: +44 (0)1494 882587

Email: info@elimhopechurch.net

Website: www.elimhopechurch.net

Facebook: www.facebook.com/elimhopechurch

Further reading

The following are books written by Arnold V Page.

Tell me about the Holy Spirit. - How to be filled with love, joy, peace and power, and extend the Kingdom of God

Available from Amazon and all good bookshops.
Books for Life Today, 2021.
Paperback 64 pages, Kindle and Epub.

Finally, here is a book that is easy to read and seeks to help the reader find ways to not just get to know the Holy Spirit, but to encounter Him. It is hard to believe that contained in such a small book a comprehensive ideology of the Holy Spirit could be so eloquently delivered. I hope you enjoy this book as much as I did.
Rev. Scott Pash - Minister of Elim Hope Church,
Lane End, Buckinghamshire

So many claim to have received the Holy Spirit, yet lack any real evidence. This book will help them to find what they are searching for.
Rev. D Hathaway DD. President Eurovision Mission to Europe

Mr Page has written a powerful book on the Holy Spirit. If you are hungry for more of God, more of his power, presence and presents, this is the resource you need.
Leke Sanusi. Head, Redeemed Christian Church of God Mission, UK.

God, Science and the Bible – Genuine Science Confirms the Bible's Amazing Message

Available from Amazon and all good bookshops.
URLink Print & Media, LLC, 2020.
Also available in Spanish: **Dios, la Ciencia y la Biblia**

Books for Life Today, 2021.
Both editions in paperback, Kindle and Epub.

Informative and life-changing.

Edith Wairimu, ReadersFavorite.com

The Date of Christ's Return – Biblical prophecy for the Final Generation

Available from Amazon and all good bookshops.
Books for Life Today, 2022.
Also available in Spanish: **La Fecha del Regreso de Cristo - Profecía Bíblica para la Generación Final**
Books for Life Today, 2022.
Both editions in paperback, Kindle and Epub.

A fascinating and remarkable portrayal of the world's entire timeline in one cohesive, panoramic form, from a Biblical perspective.

Raju Chacko for Reedsy.com

This is a good and enlightening Christian book that will transform you into a true believer of Christ.

Ekezie1998 for Online Book Club

His writing is excellent, clear, and concise. 'The Date of Christ Return' isn't a "scare tactic" but rather an encouraging reminder of the power of our faith that will sustain us for all of eternity.

Sherri Fulmer Moorer for Readers' Favorite

CPSIA information can be obtained
at www.ICGtesting.com
Printed in the USA
LVHW040309211222
735638LV00012B/332